TITLE: GOD'S CHILD BUT POOR

NOTE: ALL SCRIPTURES ARE QUOTED FROM
www.biblegateway.com

TABLE OF CONTENTS

INTRODUCTION

God is all powerful and being called his child is a privilege granted in Christ.

1st john 3:1-2

The Father has loved us so much that we are called children of God. And we really are his children. The reason the people in the world do not know us is that they have not known him. Dear friends, now we are children of God, and we have not yet been shown what we will be in the future. But we know that when Christ comes again, we will be like him, because we will see him as he really is.

This brings comfort to many believers who never had a chance to be born by rich parents or have connections with rich people. The invitation to join God's family is well received by many people with joy.

John 1:12-13

But to all who did accept him and believe in him he gave the right to become children of God. They did not become his children in any human way—by any human parents or human desire. They were born of God.

1st corinthians 1:26-29
Brothers and sisters, think of what you were when you were called. Not many of you were wise by human standards; not many were influential; not many were of noble birth. But God chose the foolish things of the world to shame the wise; God chose the weak things of the world to shame the strong.God chose the lowly things of this world and the despised things— and the things that are not—to nullify the things that are,so that no one may boast before him

However, many believers carry the title only but the privileges to show they truly belong to the king of kings are not there. This leaves many frustrated to an extent some go back to the world and those with endurance just go through life waiting to go to heaven and meet with their daddy king.

Ecclesiastes 10:5-7
There is something else wrong that happens here on earth.
    It is the kind of mistake rulers make:
Fools are given important positions
    while gifted people are given lower ones;
I have seen servants ride horses
    while princes walk like servants on foot.

This has never been God's will that his children will see the world as better than his kingdom or they suffer on earth looking for the day they enter heaven to be comforted. It is God's desire that his children enjoy life on earth.

John 10:10
A thief comes to steal, kill and destroy, but I came to give life—life in all its fullness.

3rd John 1:2
Beloved, I wish above all things that thou mayest prosper and be in health, even as thy soul prospereth.

Like rich parents give the best for their children, so the heavenly father has provided the best for his family.

Matthew 7:9-11
Which of you, if your son asks for bread, will give him a stone? Or if he asks for a fish, will give him a snake? If you, then, though you are evil, know how to give good gifts to your children, how much more will your Father in heaven give good gifts to those who ask him!

James 1:17
Every good gift and every perfect gift is from above, and comes down from the Father of lights, with whom there is no variation or shadow of turning.

 Actually, the nature of God is that he prepares all things before bringing his children on the scene. That's our daddy king!

Hebrews 4:3
Although the works were finished from the foundation of the world.

CHAPTER ONE: ADAM AND EVE

It was God's idea to make man in his image and likeness. Man was planned for by God before he brought him in the picture. Genesis 1 and 2 shows us a loving God and father who took time to create all things his children needed.

Genesis 1:1-31
In the beginning God created the heavens and the earth.The earth was without form, and void; and darkness was on the face of the deep. And the Spirit of God was hovering over the face of the waters.

Then God said, "Let there be light"; and there was light. And God saw the light, that it was good; and God divided the light from the darkness. God called the light Day, and the darkness He called Night. So the evening and the morning were the first day.

Then God said, "Let there be a firmament in the midst of the waters, and let it divide the waters from the waters."Thus God made the firmament, and divided the waters which were under the firmament from the waters which were above the firmament; and it was so. And God called the firmament Heaven. So the evening and the morning were the second day.

 Then God said, "Let the waters under the heavens be gathered together into one place, and let the dry land appear"; and it was so. And God called the dry land Earth, and the gathering together of the waters He called Seas. And God saw that it was good.

Then God said, "Let the earth bring forth grass, the herb that yields seed, and the fruit tree that yields fruit according to its kind, whose seed is in itself, on the earth"; and it was so. And the earth brought forth grass, the herb that yields seed according to its kind, and the tree that yields fruit, whose seed is in itself according to its kind. And God saw that it was good. So the evening and the morning were the third day.

Then God said, "Let there be lights in the firmament of the heavens to divide the day from the night; and let them be for signs and seasons, and for days and years; and let them be for lights in the firmament of the heavens to give light on the earth"; and it was so. Then God made two great lights: the greater light to rule the day, and the lesser light to rule the night. He made the stars also. God set them in the firmament of the heavens to give light on the earth, and to rule over the day and over the night, and to divide the light from the darkness. And God saw that it was good. So the evening and the morning were the fourth day.

Then God said, "Let the waters abound with an abundance of living creatures, and let birds fly above the earth across the face of the firmament of the heavens." So God created great sea creatures and every living thing that moved, with which the waters abounded, according to their kind, and every winged bird according to its kind. And God saw that it was good. And God blessed them, saying, "Be fruitful and multiply, and fill the waters in the seas, and let birds multiply on the earth." So the evening and the morning were the fifth day.

Then God said, "Let the earth bring forth the living creature according to its kind: cattle and creeping thing and beast of the earth, each according to its kind"; and it was so. And God made the beast of the earth according to its kind, cattle according to its kind, and everything that creeps on the earth according to its kind. And God saw that it was good.

Then God said, "Let Us make man in Our image, according to Our likeness; let them have dominion over the fish of the sea, over the birds of the air, and over the cattle, over all the earth and over every creeping thing that creeps on the earth." So God created man in His own image; in the image of God He created him; male and female He created them. Then God blessed them, and God said to them, "Be fruitful and multiply; fill the earth and subdue it; have dominion over the fish of the sea, over the birds of the air, and over every living thing that moves on the earth."

And God said, "See, I have given you every herb that yields seed which is on the face of all the earth, and every tree whose fruit yields seed; to you it shall be for food. Also, to every beast of the earth, to every bird of the air, and to everything that creeps on the earth, in which there is life, I have given every green herb for food"; and it was so. Then God saw everything that He had made, and indeed it was very good. So the evening and the morning were the sixth day.

When God saw that all was available, then he created man as the last thing to enjoy all he had made. Adam found all things were provided and all he needed to do was just fellowship with

God and manage what God had created. God even created a woman to help him as he enjoyed his wife's companionship. Adam was the god of the world. What a restful life and a loving father.

Genesis 2:1-25

Thus the heavens and the earth, and all the host of them, were finished. And on the seventh day God ended His work which He had done, and He rested on the seventh day from all His work which He had done.Then God blessed the seventh day and sanctified it, because in it He rested from all His work which God had created and made.

This is the history of the heavens and the earth when they were created, on the day that the Lord God made the earth and the heavens, before any plant of the field was in the earth and before any herb of the field had grown. For the Lord God had not caused it to rain on the earth, and there was no man to till the ground; but a mist went up from the earth and watered the whole face of the ground.

And the Lord God formed man of the dust of the ground, and breathed into his nostrils the breath of life; and man became a living being.

The Lord God planted a garden eastward in Eden, and there He put the man whom He had formed. And out of the ground the Lord God made every tree grow that is pleasant to the sight and good for food. The tree of life was also in the midst of the garden, and the tree of the knowledge of good and evil.

Now a river went out of Eden to water the garden, and from there it parted and became four riverheads. The name of the first is Pishon; it is the one which skirts the whole land of Havilah, where there is gold. And the gold of that land is good. Bdellium and the onyx stone are there. The name of the second river is Gihon; it is the one which goes around the whole land of Cush. The name of the third river is Hiddekel; it is the one which goes toward the east of Assyria. The fourth river is the Euphrates.

Then the Lord God took the man and put him in the garden of Eden to tend and keep it. And the Lord God commanded the man, saying, "Of every tree of the garden you may freely eat; but of the tree of the knowledge of good and evil you shall not eat, for on the day that you eat of it you shall surely die."

And the Lord God said, "It is not good that man should be alone; I will make him a helper comparable to him." Out of the ground the Lord God formed every beast of the field and every bird of the air, and brought them to Adam to see what he would call them. And whatever Adam called each living creature, that was its name. So Adam gave names to all cattle, to the birds of the air, and to every beast of the field. But for Adam there was not found a helper comparable to him.

And the Lord God caused a deep sleep to fall on Adam, and he slept; and He took one of his ribs, and closed up the flesh in its place. Then the rib which the Lord God had taken from man He made into a woman, and He brought her to the man.

And Adam said:

"This is now bone of my bones

And flesh of my flesh;
She shall be called Woman,
Because she was taken out of Man.”

Therefore a man shall leave his father and mother and be joined to his wife, and they shall become one flesh.
And they were both naked, the man and his wife, and were not ashamed.

Adam fell from his glorious position because of ignorance.

Hosea 4:6
my people are destroyed from lack of knowledge.

“Because you have rejected knowledge,
    I also reject you as my priests;
because you have ignored the law of your God,
    I also will ignore your children.

Psalms 82:5-7
The ‘gods’ know nothing, they understand nothing.
    They walk about in darkness;
    all the foundations of the earth are shaken.

“I said, ‘You are “gods”;
    you are all sons of the Most High.’
But you will die like mere mortals;
    you will fall like every other ruler.

He had not known that he was in God's image for if he did, the devil would not have taken advantage of him.

John 8:31-32
Then Jesus said to those Jews who believed Him, "If you abide in My word, you are My disciples indeed. And you shall know the truth, and the truth shall make you free."

2nd Corinthians 2:11
To keep Satan from taking advantage of us; for we are not ignorant of his schemes.

Satan showed him and his wife that they were not like God and if they ate the fruit from the tree God commanded them not to eat, they would become like God.

Genesis 3:1-7
 Now the serpent was more crafty than any of the wild animals the Lord God had made. He said to the woman, "Did God really say, 'You must not eat from any tree in the garden'?"
 The woman said to the serpent, "We may eat fruit from the trees in the garden, but God did say, 'You must not eat fruit from the tree that is in the middle of the garden, and you must not touch it, or you will die.'"
 "You will not certainly die," **the serpent said to the woman. "For God knows that when you eat from it your eyes will be opened, and you will be like God, knowing good and evil."**

When the woman saw that the fruit of the tree was good for food and pleasing to the eye, and also desirable for gaining wisdom, she took some and ate it. **She also gave some to her husband, who was with her, and he ate it. Then the eyes of both of them were opened, and they realised they were naked; so they sewed fig leaves together and made coverings for themselves.**

Genesis 3:16-23
To the woman He said:

"I will greatly multiply your sorrow and your conception;
In pain you shall bring forth children;
Your desire shall be for your husband,
And he shall rule over you."
 Then to Adam He said, "Because you have heeded the voice of your wife, and have eaten from the tree of which I commanded you, saying, 'You shall not eat of it':

"Cursed is the ground for your sake;
In toil you shall eat of it
All the days of your life.
 Both thorns and thistles it shall bring forth for you,
And you shall eat the herb of the field.
In the sweat of your face you shall eat bread
Till you return to the ground,
For out of it you were taken;
For dust you are,
And to dust you shall return."

And Adam called his wife's name Eve,because she was the mother of all living.

Also for Adam and his wife the Lord God made tunics of skin, and clothed them.

Then the Lord God said, "Behold, the man has become like one of Us, to know good and evil. And now, lest he put out his hand and take also of the tree of life, and eat, and live forever" therefore **the Lord God sent him out of the garden of Eden to till the ground from which he was taken.**

Ignorance made them lose all to Satan who became the god of this world.

Luke 4:5-8

Then the devil, taking Him up on a high mountain, showed Him all the kingdoms of the world in a moment of time.And the devil said to Him, "**All this authority I will give You, and their glory; for this has been delivered to me, and I give it to whomever I wish.** Therefore, if You will worship before me, all will be Yours."

And Jesus answered and said to him, "Get behind Me, Satan! For it is written, 'You shall worship the Lord your God, and Him only you shall serve.'"

2nd Corinthians 4:4

Satan, who is the god of this world, has blinded the minds of those who don't believe. They are unable to see the glorious light of the Good News. They don't understand this message about the glory of Christ, who is the exact likeness of God.

CHAPTER TWO: THE ISRAELITES
God made a covenant with his friend Abraham to take care of his generations for Abraham obeyed him. When the children of Abraham cried to God in slavery, God prepared a place of freedom and abundance before he came to deliver them.

Exodus 2:23-24
During that long period, the king of Egypt died. The Israelites groaned in their slavery and cried out, and their cry for help because of their slavery went up to God. God heard their groaning and he remembered his covenant with Abraham, with Isaac and with Jacob.

God described the land he had prepared for them as one flowing with milk and honey. A land with houses they had not built that God made other people to build, crops they had not planted etc.

Exodus 3:7-9
And the Lord said: "I have surely seen the oppression of My people who are in Egypt, and have heard their cry because of their taskmasters, for I know their sorrows. So I have come down to deliver them out of the hand of the Egyptians, and to bring them up from that land to a good and large land, to a land flowing with milk and honey, to the place of the Canaanites and the Hittites and the

Amorites and the Perizzites and the Hivites and the Jebusites. Now therefore, behold, the cry of the children of Israel has come to Me, and I have also seen the oppression with which the Egyptians oppress them."

Deuteronomy 6:10-13
"So it shall be, when the Lord your God brings you into the land of which He swore to your fathers, to Abraham, Isaac, and Jacob, **to give you large and beautiful cities which you did not build, houses full of all good things, which you did not fill, hewn-out wells which you did not dig, vineyards and olive trees which you did not plant—when you have eaten and are full,** then beware, lest you forget the Lord who brought you out of the land of Egypt, from the house of bondage. You shall fear the Lord your God and serve Him, and shall take oaths in His name.

It was God's plan to get them out of Egypt into Canaan not let them die in the wilderness like many did. Satan took advantage of the Israelites like he did of Adam. They didn't see like God saw. When God saw them in Canaan, they saw themselves going back to Egypt/slavery or dying in the wilderness. They didn't believe God's plan for them and their lack of faith in God saw them dead.

Hebrews 11:6

And without faith it is impossible to please God, because anyone who comes to him must believe that he exists and that he rewards those who earnestly seek him.

Their words could tell what they were believing. Out of a whole nation that came out of Egypt, only two people, Joshua and Caleb entered the land God had promised.
They chose to believe God's word which changed their thinking and even their talking. They may have been born as slaves but they believed God's word that they were home owners and prosperous.

Numbers 14:1-4
So all the congregation lifted up their voices and cried, and the people wept that night. **And all the children of Israel complained against Moses and Aaron, and the whole congregation said to them, "If only we had died in the land of Egypt! Or if only we had died in this wilderness!** Why has the Lord brought us to this land to fall by the sword, that our wives and children should become victims? Would it not be better for us to return to Egypt?" So they said to one another, "Let us select a leader and return to Egypt."

Deuteronomy 14:26-35
And the Lord spoke to Moses and Aaron, saying, "How long shall I bear with this evil congregation who complain against Me? I have heard the complaints which the children of Israel make against Me. Say to them, 'As I live,' says the Lord, 'just as you have spoken in My hearing, so I will do to you: **The**

carcasses of you who have complained against Me shall fall in this wilderness, all of you who were numbered, according to your entire number, from twenty years old and above. Except for Caleb the son of Jephunneh and Joshua the son of Nun, you shall by no means enter the land which I swore I would make you dwell in. *But your little ones, whom you said would be victims, I will bring in, and they shall know the land which you have <u>despised</u>.* But as for you, your carcasses shall fall in this wilderness. And your sons shall be shepherds in the wilderness forty years, and bear the brunt of your infidelity, until your carcasses are consumed in the wilderness.According to the number of the days in which you spied out the land, forty days, for each day you shall bear your guilt one year, namely forty years, and you shall know My rejection. I the Lord have spoken this. I will surely do so to all this evil congregation who are gathered together against Me. In this wilderness they shall be consumed, and there they shall die.' "

CHAPTER THREE: JESUS CHRIST

God stepped on earth to take back what Satan stole from Adam. Since the fall of Adam, Satan ruled the world with poverty and many suffered. Only those who believed in God lived in prosperity.

Matthew 28:18-20

Then Jesus came to them and said, "All authority in heaven and on earth has been given to me. Therefore go and make

disciples of all nations, baptising them in the name of the Father and of the Son and of the Holy Spirit, and teaching them to obey everything I have commanded you. And surely I am with you always, to the very end of the age."

Jesus lived a life of abundance on earth. He proved that God's kingdom is full of provisions for his children.

Matthew 25:34
Then shall the King say unto them on His right hand, 'Come, ye blessed of My Father, inherit the Kingdom prepared for you from the foundation of the world.

Jesus was never stranded in any situation, he made the provisions available to meet all the needs as they arose.

Philippians 4:19
And my God shall supply all your need according to His riches in glory by Christ Jesus.

He showed that indeed he had come that we have life and have it to the fullest.
When people were hungry, he fed all of them and there were left overs.

Mark 6:34-44
When Jesus landed and saw a large crowd, he had compassion on them, because they were like sheep without a shepherd. So he began teaching them many things.

By this time it was late in the day, so his disciples came to him. "This is a remote place," they said, "and it's already very late. Send the people away so that they can go to the surrounding countryside and villages and buy themselves something to eat." But he answered, "You give them something to eat."
They said to him, "That would take more than half a year's wages! Are we to go and spend that much on bread and give it to them to eat?"
 "How many loaves do you have?" he asked. "Go and see." When they found out, they said, "Five—and two fish." Then Jesus directed them to have all the people sit down in groups on the green grass. So they sat down in groups of hundreds and fifties. Taking the five loaves and the two fish and looking up to heaven, he gave thanks and broke the loaves. Then he gave them to his disciples to distribute to the people. He also divided the two fish among them all. **They all ate and were satisfied, and the disciples picked up twelve basketfuls of broken pieces of bread and fish. The number of the men who had eaten was five thousan**d.

When tax collectors needed their money, he provided and stopped shame from coming on him and his ministry.

Matthew 17:24-27
When they had come to Capernaum, those who received the temple tax came to Peter and said, "Does your Teacher not pay the temple tax?"
 He said, "Yes."

And when he had come into the house, Jesus anticipated him, saying, "What do you think, Simon? From whom do the kings of the earth take customs or taxes, from their sons or from strangers?"

Peter said to Him, "From strangers."

Jesus said to him, "Then the sons are free. Nevertheless, lest we offend them, **go to the sea, cast in a hook, and take the fish that comes up first. And when you have opened its mouth, you will find a piece of money; take that and give it to them for Me and you."**

When Peter was in a financial crisis, he provided for him and his partners until they left all and followed him.

Luke 5:1-11

One day as Jesus was standing by the Lake of Gennesaret,the people were crowding around him and listening to the word of God.He saw at the water's edge two boats, left there by the fishermen, who were washing their nets. He got into one of the boats, the one belonging to Simon, and asked him to put out a little from shore. Then he sat down and taught the people from the boat.

When he had finished speaking, he said to Simon, "Put out into deep water, and let down the nets for a catch."

Simon answered, "Master, we've worked hard all night and haven't caught anything. But because you say so, I will let down the net."

When they had done so, **they caught such a large number of fish that their net began to break. So they signalled their**

partners in the other boat to come and help them, and they came and filled both boats so full that they began to sink.
 When Simon Peter saw this, he fell at Jesus' knees and said, "Go away from me, Lord; I am a sinful man!" For he and all his companions were astonished at the catch of fish they had taken, and so were James and John, the sons of Zebedee, Simon's partners.
Then Jesus said to Simon, "Don't be afraid; from now on you will fish for people." So they pulled their boats up on shore, left everything and followed him.

On the cross, he took that curse(power) satan had put on people that brought poverty. Today, all those who believe in Jesus, the father has put the blessing(power) on them that brings riches.

2nd corinthians 8:9
For you know the grace of our Lord Jesus Christ, that though he was rich, yet for your sake he became poor, so that you through his poverty might become rich.

Ephesians 1:3
For you know the grace of our Lord Jesus Christ, that though he was rich, yet for your sake he became poor, so that you through his poverty might become rich.

Proverbs 10:22
The blessing of the Lord makes one rich,
And He adds no sorrow with it.

The father in Christ has given his children all things they need to live a good and godly life.

2nd peter 1:3
According as his divine power hath given unto us all things that pertain unto life and godliness, through the knowledge of him that hath called us to glory and virtue.

However, most children of God in the physical are experiencing lack, scarcity and living a life with no Glory of God. Even if the father intended to use his children to showcase his wisdom, many believers have made the devil to mock God.

Ephesians 3:10
God's purpose in all this was to use the church to display his wisdom in its rich variety to all the unseen rulers and authorities in the heavenly places.

Romans 2:24
No wonder the Scriptures say, "The Gentiles blaspheme the name of God because of you."

It's time to arise and showcase the glory of our father, manifest what he did before the foundation of the world and on the cross.

Isaiah 60:1
Arise, shine, for your light has come,
   and the glory of the Lord rises upon you.

Jesus is the one who knows the cost of our prosperity and he is
alive to ensure that we get that which he paid for us.

Hebrews 9:15-17
For this reason Christ brings a new agreement from God to his
people. Those who are called by God can now receive the
blessings he has promised, blessings that will last forever. They
can have those things because Christ died so that the people
who lived under the first agreement could be set free from sin.
When there is a will, it must be proven that the one who wrote
that will is dead. A will means nothing while the person is
alive; it can be used only after the person dies.

CHAPTER FOUR: BELIEVERS RESPONSIBILITY
God is a spirit and the spirit world is as real as the physical
world. Actually, the spirit world created the physical world.
On the side of God, everything concerning your life as his child
is provided. Your life is planned for already and all you will
ever need has been released in the spirit world.

John 4:24
God is a Spirit.

2nd corinthians 4:18

while we look not at the things which are seen, but at the things which are not seen. For the things which are seen are temporal, but the things which are not seen are eternal.

Hebrews 11:3
By faith we understand that the universe was formed at God's command, so that what is seen was not made out of what was visible.

Jeremiah 29:11
For I know the plans I have for you," declares the Lord, "plans to prosper you and not to harm you, plans to give you hope and a future.

Psalms 139:16
Your eyes saw my unformed body;
   all the days ordained for me were written in your book
   before one of them came to be.

It's your responsibility to convert the spiritual into the physical. This is where the devil takes advantage of many believers for they don't know. Have you seen that ignorance is very dangerous? When God saw darkness, he called forth light. You need the word of God to give you light. Your prosperity is not all dependent on God, you have a part to play.

Job 38:33
Do you know the laws of the heavens? Can you set their dominion over the earth?

God created each of us with abilities but most believers have acted like the foolish servant, they have hidden them. Every child of God has something given to them that they can use in the world and get rewarded with money or the form of exchange available for the value they offer.

Ephesians 4:7
But unto every one of us is given grace according to the measure of the gift of Christ.

However, either believers don't know and those who know have despised what they have.
When the master went, he gave talents to his servants according to their abilities. The one with five talents multiplied them into ten and he was commended for that by his master. The one who received two also valued them and multiplied them into two more. Unfortunately, the one with one hid it and insulted his master. He didn't attach any value to what he was given and dishonoured the giver. This caused him to be demoted.

Matthew 25:14-30
For it will be like a man going on a journey, who called his servants and entrusted to them his property. To one he gave five talents, to another two, to another one, to each according to his ability. Then he went away. He who had received the five talents went at once and traded with them, and

he made five talents more. So also he who had the two talents made two talents more. But he who had received the one talent went and dug in the ground and hid his master's money. Now after a long time the master of those servants came and settled accounts with them. And he who had received the five talents came forward, bringing five talents more, saying, **'Master, you delivered to me five talents; here, I have made five talents more.' His master said to him, 'Well done, good and faithful servant. You have been faithful over a little; I will set you over much.** Enter into the joy of your master.' And he also who had the two talents came forward, saying, 'Master, you delivered to me two talents; here, I have made two talents more.' His master said to him, 'Well done, good and faithful servant. You have been faithful over a little; I will set you over much. Enter into the joy of your master.' **He also who had received the one talent came forward, saying, 'Master, I knew you to be a hard man, reaping where you did not sow, and gathering where you scattered no seed, so I was afraid, and I went and hid your talent in the ground. Here, you have what is yours.' But his master answered him, 'You wicked and slothful servant! You knew that I reap where I have not sown and gather where I scattered no seed? Then you ought to have invested my money with the bankers, and at my coming I should have received what was my own with interest. So take the talent from him and give it to him who has the ten talents. For to everyone who has will more be given, and he will have an abundance. But from the one who has not, even what he has will be taken away. And**

cast the worthless servant into the outer darkness. In that place there will be weeping and gnashing of teeth.'

Like the widow who came to the prophet crying because of debts but despised the little oil in her house, so are many believers. The oil she despised was what got her out of debt. The husband died in poverty while the oil had been in the house all that time.

2nd kings 4:1-7
the wife of a man from the company of the prophets cried out to Elisha, "Your servant my husband is dead, and you know that he revered the Lord. But now his creditor is coming to take my two boys as his slaves."
 Elisha replied to her, "How can I help you? Tell me, what do you have in your house?"
"Your servant has nothing there at all," she said, **"except a small jar of olive oil."**
 Elisha said, "Go around and ask all your neighbours for empty jars. Don't ask for just a few. Then go inside and shut the door behind you and your sons. Pour oil into all the jars, and as each is filled, put it to one side."
She left him and shut the door behind her and her sons. **They brought the jars to her and she kept pouring. When all the jars were full, she said to her son, "Bring me another one."**
But he replied, "There is not a jar left." Then the oil stopped flowing.

She went and told the man of God, and he said, "**Go, sell the oil and pay your debts. You and your sons can live on what is left.**"

David didn't despise the stone in his hand and God used it to bring down goliath.

1st kings 40:51
Then he took his staff in his hand, choose five smooth stones from the stream, put them in the pouch of his shepherd's bag and, with his sling in his hand, approached the Philistine. Meanwhile, the Philistine, with his shield bearer in front of him, kept coming closer to David. **He looked David over and saw that he was little more than a boy, glowing with health and handsome, and he despised him.** He said to David, "Am I a dog, that you come at me with sticks?" And the Philistine cursed David by his gods. "Come here," he said, "and I'll give your flesh to the birds and the wild animals!"
David said to the Philistine, "You come against me with sword and spear and javelin, but I come against you in the name of the Lord Almighty, the God of the armies of Israel, whom you have defied. This day the Lord will deliver you into my hands, and I'll strike you down and cut off your head. This very day I will give the carcasses of the Philistine army to the birds and the wild animals, and the whole world will know that there is a God in Israel. **All those gathered here will know that it is not by sword or spear that the Lord saves;**

for the battle is the Lord's, and he will give all of you into our hands."

As the Philistine moved closer to attack him, **David ran quickly toward the battle line to meet him. Reaching into his bag and taking out a stone, he slung it and struck the Philistine on the forehead. The stone sank into his forehead, and he fell facedown on the ground.**

So David triumphed over the Philistine with a sling and a stone; without a sword in his hand he struck down the Philistine and killed him.

David ran and stood over him. He took hold of the Philistine's sword and drew it from the sheath. After he killed him, he cut off his head with the sword.

Whatever grace the lord has given you, don't frustrate it. There is that area that you are so good at, focus on it and develop it. For example, business, governance, music, writing, education, football, etc.

Galatians 2:21

I do not frustrate the grace of God: for if righteousness come by the law, then Christ is dead in vain.

Paul was called to be an apostle and he didn't frustrate the Grace of God upon his life. He took advantage of that grace and became the greatest among all apostles. Paul overtook peter and other disciples who had been with Jesus while he was on earth and had seen him when he resurrected.

1st Corinthians 15:9-10

For I am the least of the apostles, that am not meet to be called an apostle, because I persecuted the church of God. **But by the grace of God I am what I am: and his grace which was bestowed upon me was not in vain;** but I laboured more abundantly than they all: yet not I, but the grace of God which was with me.

It doesn't matter what disadvantage you may have against the people in the world. There is an advantage of God's grace in your life. Depend on the holy spirit to help you discover it and apply excellence to it. You have the backup of the God who gave you that grace, take steps of faith and start to use it.

2nd Corinthians 12:9

But he said to me, "My grace is sufficient for you, for my power is made perfect in weakness." Therefore I will boast all the more gladly about my weaknesses, so that Christ's power may rest on me.

What you have may look small and to be despised but remember that God uses the weak and despised things to glorify himself. When you are living that glorious life you will know that it was God who was with you in the whole journey.

Philippians 2:13

for it is God who works in you both to will and to do for His good pleasure.

Joseph had a gift of interpreting dreams. It didn't look like something big but he used it where God provided opportunity. He didn't despise it and God made sure that gift took him from prison to the palace.

Genesis 41:14-16
Then Pharaoh sent and called Joseph, and they brought him quickly out of the dungeon; and he shaved, changed his clothing, and came to Pharaoh. And Pharaoh said to Joseph, "I have had a dream, and there is no one who can interpret it. But I have heard it said of you that you can understand a dream, to interpret it."
So Joseph answered Pharaoh, saying, "It is not in me; God will give Pharaoh an answer of peace."

Genesis 41:39-40
Then Pharaoh said to Joseph, "Since God has made all this known to you, there is no one so discerning and wise as you. You shall be in charge of my palace, and all my people are to submit to your orders. Only with respect to the throne will I be greater than you."

Isaiah 60:3
The Gentiles shall come to your light,
And kings to the brightness of your rising.

Zechariah 4:10
For who has despised the day of small things?

Job 8:7
Though thy beginning was small, yet thy latter end should greatly increase.

Proverbs 18:16
A person's gift makes room for him And brings him before great people.

Proverbs 22:29
Do you see a man who excels in his work? He will stand before kings; He will not stand before unknown men.

JOHN 13:17
NOW THAT YOU KNOW THESE THINGS, YOU WILL BE BLESSED IF YOU DO THEM.

More grace on you as you convert the spiritual blessings into physical provisions and showcase God's glory as his child.

If you need help to study God's word, email me at pstmaryjoy@gmail.com and I will guide you through.

To get my other books in amazon, click this link
https://www.amazon.com/author/marynyandia